Swedish AMERICANS

SPIRIT
of America®

Swedish Americans

By Lucia Raatma

The Child's World®
Chanhassen, Minnesota

6

Swedish AMERICANS

Published in the United States of America by The Child's World®
PO Box 326 • Chanhassen, MN 55317-0326 • 800-599-READ • www.childsworld.com

Acknowledgments

The Child's World®: Mary Berendes, Publishing Director

Editorial Directions, Inc.: E. Russell Primm, Emily Dolbear, Sarah E. De Capua, and Lucia Raatma, Editors; Linda S. Koutris, Photo Selector; Image Select International, Photo Research; Red Line Editorial and Pam Rosenberg, Fact Research; Tim Griffin/IndexServ, Indexer; Chad Rubel, Proofreader

Photos

Cover/frontispiece: A Swedish-American family entertaining a soldier for Sunday dinner, Minnesota, 1942

Cover photographs ©: Library of Congress; Imagestate

Interior photographs ©: Corbis, 6; Ann Ronan Picture Library, 7, 8; Corbis, 9, 10, New York Public Library, 11; AKG-Images, Berlin, 12; 13 top; Corbis, 13 bottom, 14, AKG-Images, Berlin, 15, 16; Cranbrook Academy, 17 top; Corbis, 17 bottom; Culver Pictures, 18; Corbis, 19; Ann Ronan Picture Library, 20 top; Getty Images, 20 bottom; Cinema Bookshop, 21 top; AKG-Images, Berlin, 21 centre; Getty Images, 21 bottom; AKG-Images, Berlin, 23; Getty Images, 24; 25 top; Ann Ronan Picture Library, 26 top; Corbis, 26 bottom, 27 top; Culver Pictures, 27 bottom; Getty Images, 28.

Library of Congress Cataloging-in-Publication Data
Raatma, Lucia.
  Swedish Americans / by Lucia Raatma.
      p. cm.
  Includes index.
  Summary: A brief introduction to Swedish Americans, their historical backgrounds, customs, and traditions, their impact on society, and life in the United States today.
  ISBN 1-56766-159-9 (lib. bdg. : alk. paper)
  1. Swedish Americans—Juvenile literature. [1. Swedish Americans.] I. Title.
  E184.S23 R33 2002
  973'.04397—dc21
                          2001007809

12   18   28

Contents

Chapter ONE	*The Swedish Life*	6
Chapter TWO	*Coming to America*	12
Chapter THREE	*Making a New Home*	18
Chapter FOUR	*The Swedish-American Culture*	24
	Time Line	29
	Glossary Terms	30
	For Further Information	31
	Index	32

The Swedish Life

THE HISTORY OF AMERICA IS CLOSELY TIED TO the people of Sweden. As early as 1638, Swedes came to the American colonies and formed a settlement called New Sweden. This community in Delaware lasted only until 1655, when the Dutch gained control over it. But the people of New Sweden remained, and their **descendants** went on to fight in the Revolutionary War (1775–1783) and help win their freedom from Great Britain.

Shortly after the Revolutionary War, Sweden played another important role for

The founders of New Sweden landing in Delaware in 1638 and being greeted by Native Americans

America. Just after Great Britain was defeated in the war, King Gustav III of Sweden arranged a meeting between an ambassador from Sweden and Benjamin Franklin. The Swedish ambassador and Franklin worked on a treaty that encouraged friendship and trade between their two countries. That gesture by Sweden showed that the new country of the United States of America was being taken seriously by the rest of the world.

King Gustav III of Sweden, an early friend to the new country of the United States

In the years to come, Swedes would bring even more to the American way of life. During the 19th century, many of them chose to make America their home. And with that decision, America was blessed by a strong, hardworking group of people who brought wonderful traditions, food, and culture to the young nation.

The 1800s proved to be a time of great change in Sweden. During the **Napoleonic Wars**,

▶ More than 1.3 million Swedes moved to the United States between 1840 and 1930. In 1800, about 2.3 million people lived in Sweden. By 1910, the Swedish population had grown to about 5.5 million.

The Napoleonic Wars brought about great change in Sweden.

Sweden had briefly formed an **alliance** with Russia and Great Britain. This alliance was meant to protect them from Napoléon Bonaparte and his French forces. But when Russia invaded Finland in 1807, the alliance turned bad for Sweden. Two years later, Sweden lost to Russia the land that it held in Finland, in addition to some of its own land. This loss was a terrible blow to the Swedish people, and they were angry with King Gustav IV for letting it happen. The king was forced from power, and a new Constitution was adopted. This Constitution called for government reform and increased the power of the people.

The changes in government were good ones for Sweden, but other problems remained. After the Napoleonic Wars ended in 1815, the Swedish economy was poor. Many people lived in poverty, there was not enough land to farm, and the Swedes felt the land taxes were unfair. In addition, all Swedish men were required to serve in the military. Though these military assignments were brief—usually four to six weeks—Swedes believed that these requirements invaded their personal lives.

A group of female Pietists at a Sunday afternoon gathering

The Swedish people were also dissatisfied with government control of religion. Most Swedes belonged to the Lutheran Church, but there were other groups as well. For example, the Pietists broke away from the Lutherans and believed that personal experience with religion was more important than the official church. At one point, the government passed a law forbidding any religious meetings that were not controlled by the official church. Though this law was eventually reversed in 1858, the state

Families moving to the American West in the late 1800s

church remained very powerful.

As medical care in Sweden improved, more people lived longer. As a result, the nation's shortage of farmland became even more of a problem. Large families had to split up their land among a number of sons, or some of the sons had to leave and find work elsewhere. Also, a period of bad weather ruined much of the crops. **Droughts** and floods took their toll on the fields, resulting in disappointing harvests—and hunger.

In the meantime, people in the United States were beginning to move west. Acres and acres of farmland there were just waiting to be cleared and settled. The Swedes saw America as a nation of opportunity—a place with plentiful land, religious freedom, and a **democratic** government. Slowly at first, and then with increasing speed, many Swedish people began crossing the Atlantic for a new life in America.

10

ONE IMPORTANT SWEDISH IMMIGRANT TO THE UNITED STATES WAS Gustav Unonius. He came to America in 1841 with his wife, Charlotte. They landed in New York, then traveled to the Midwest by way of the Hudson River, the Erie Canal, and then the Great Lakes. Once in Wisconsin, Unonius and his wife and some friends settled in New Uppsala, an area about 30 miles (48 kilometers) from Milwaukee.

Unonius was charmed by the beauty of New Uppsala, and he wrote many letters to friends in Sweden. In these letters, he praised the abundance of land and the natural splendor he found all around him. At first, the letters were passed from house to house, but then they were also published in the Swedish papers. The words of Unonius influenced thousands of people, who then decided to give America a try.

Gustav Unonius went on to become a minister and served communities in Wisconsin and Chicago. After 17 years in America, however, he found himself exhausted and returned to Sweden. There he published his **memoirs** in which he criticized some Americans for their treatment of immigrants. But mostly he wrote about the opportunities to be found in the United States. He praised the beauty of the plains and the democracy of the government, but he warned that only the strong and the determined could succeed in the new land.

Chapter Two

Coming to America

BEGINNING IN THE 1840S, THE SWEDISH PEOPLE began making the voyage to America. At that time, the journey was quite dangerous and could take months. **Immigrants** traveled on large cargo ships and were often weak and ill by the time they landed in New York. After the Civil War (1861–1865), immigrants began arriving on more modern ocean liners. These ships were still crowded and unpleasant, but the trip was quicker, usually taking only two to three weeks.

Immigrants boarding a ship heading to the United States in 1875

The Swedish immigrants arrived on ships that docked in New York Harbor. Initially, these and other immigrants were welcomed at Castle Garden, a port of entry located on the southern tip of Manhattan. As more and more immigrants arrived in America, Castle Garden could not handle them all. So in 1892, Ellis Island became the official immigrant port of entry. Newcomers to America were questioned, examined, and processed there.

For most Swedish Americans, New York

Castle Garden, where immigrants were processed prior to 1892

Swedish Americans marching through Boston before heading to the West

was just a stopping point. After landing there, most headed for the Midwest and the West. At first, these trips were made by boat. Immigrants boarded paddle steamers that took them up the Hudson River to Albany. From there, other boats took them across the Great Lakes to the cities of Chicago, Illinois; Duluth, Minnesota; and Milwaukee, Wisconsin. By the mid-1850s, however, railroads had been built, so the newcomers could board a train in New York and go straight to Chicago.

Many Swedish Americans settled in areas like this one near Grafton, North Dakota.

Some Swedish Americans stayed in the cities, becoming factory workers in Chicago or housekeepers in Milwaukee. But many of them were lured to the open plains. The Homestead Act of 1862 gave free land—160 acres (65 hectares)—to each person willing to settle in Minnesota and other states farther west. Settling new land was a difficult task,

Interesting Fact

▶ For a time, Chicago had the second-largest Swedish population of any city in the world, after Stockholm.

14

The Swedish city of Stockholm in 1881

but many Swedes were eager for the challenge.

By the mid-1870s, the number of Swedish immigrants decreased slightly. Many areas of industry improved in Sweden, so fewer people felt the need to leave the country. But by 1880, another wave of immigration began. These were primarily people from Swedish cities, especially Stockholm. Cities in Sweden were becoming more and more crowded, and many people could not find jobs. These Swedes saw opportunity in American cities such as New York and Boston. They came to America to work in factories and other urban industries.

By the beginning of the 20th century, the number of Swedish immigrants slowed down again. Sweden was trying to improve its working conditions, and the country needed a lot of workers for its industries. Also, during World War I (1914–1918), few people wanted to risk traveling across the Atlantic Ocean where ships were often engaged in battle. After the war, a

Interesting Fact

▶ Many Swedish Americans decided to "Americanize" their names, so Bengtson became Benson and Nilsson became Nelson, while Esbjörn became Osborn and Svenson became Swanson.

15

brief increase took place in immigration, peaking in 1923. But when the **Great Depression** began in 1929, that wave of immigration came to an abrupt end. Those already in the United States faced poverty and unemployment, so the former "land of opportunity" had lost its appeal for newcomers.

The Great Depression was hard on Americans of all backgrounds.

16

CARL MILLES, AN ARTIST WHO was born in Lagga, Sweden, came to the United States in 1929. The sculptor was intrigued by running water and his love of nature led him to create some of the most beautiful outdoor fountains in the United States and Sweden. Among them are *Meeting of the Waters* (below) in St. Louis, Missouri, and *Fountain of Faith* in Falls Church, Virginia.

Milles's *Fountain of the Muses* was exhibited at the Metropolitan Museum of Art in New York City for many years before being purchased by Brookgreen Gardens, an outdoor sculpture garden in South Carolina.

Milles's work is also on display at New York's Rockefeller Center and at Cranbrook Academy of Art in Bloomfield Hills, Michigan, a school where he taught for many years. His Swedish home in Lidingo, near Stockholm, has been transformed into Millesgärden, a museum and garden open to the public.

17

Chapter THREE

Making a New Home

UPON ARRIVING IN THE UNITED STATES, MANY Swedish-American immigrants faced disappointment and fear. Sometimes they could not find jobs they had expected, and sometimes they missed Sweden and the people they left behind. But, more often than not, these determined people overcame the problems they faced. They built new houses, worked farms, and started businesses, knowing that they were bettering their lives.

Swedish Americans used their determination to work farms throughout the United States.

Many Swedish Americans contributed to the settling of the American West and made their living as farmers. A large number of Swedes moved to American cities, however, especially Chicago—a city some say was built by the Swedish population. Many immigrants congregated in a part of the city called Swede Town.

Groups of Swedes formed communities

Many Swedes kept their traditions while embracing the American lifestyle.

throughout the Midwest, including the cities of Minneapolis and Milwaukee. They built churches, schools, and social clubs. Today, many cities and towns throughout the United States boast a large Swedish-American population.

Once they arrived in the United States, many Swedish Americans started newspapers. Some of these papers, such as *Hemlandet*, were printed in Swedish and encouraged the preservation of Swedish customs in America. Others, such as *Svenska Amerikanare*, urged

John Ericcson, a Swedish-American designer of ships

Walter Hoving while chairman of Tiffany & Company in 1955

Swedes to adopt American ways of life. Journals such as *Valkyrian* and *Präireblomman* published poetry and articles by Swedish Americans. One particularly successful Swedish American was John Ericsson. He was born in the Varmland Province of Sweden and came to the United States in 1839. As a boy, Ericsson was a good mechanic, and as he grew older, he built engines and boilers. He was the first to use screw propellers instead of paddle wheels on ships. While living in London in the early 1830s, Ericsson built the first commercial ship to use a propeller. Once in the United States, Ericsson designed a variety of ships. Among them were the *Princeton*, the first warship to use a propeller, and the *Monitor*, one of the first warships made of iron. This ship was involved in a famous Civil War battle with the *Merrimac*, another ironclad warship.

Other Swedes who made names for themselves in the United States include Carl Swanson, who invented the TV dinner, and Walter Hoving, who was chairman of the board of Tiffany & Company and then president of Lord & Taylor department store. Joe Hill, who was born in Sweden as Joel Emmanuel Häglund, was a controversial **union activist** in America.

A number of Swedish-American actresses have made an impression on U.S. audiences. Greta Garbo was born in Stockholm and moved to America where she starred in *Grand Hotel* and other films. Ingrid Bergman was also born in Stockholm, but she came to America in her 20s and went on to make movies such as *Casablanca* and *Gaslight*. Ann-Margret was born Ann-Margret Olsson in a small Swedish village called Valsjobyn. She moved to America at age five and later starred in such films as *Bye-Bye Birdie*, *State Fair*, and *Tommy*.

Swedish-American actresses Greta Garbo (above), Ingrid Bergman (left), and Ann-Margret (below)

St. Lucia's Day

ACCORDING TO SWEDISH TRADITION, THE CHRISTMAS SEASON BEGINS on December 13, Saint Lucia's Day. At dawn on this day, a daughter in each family wears a long, white gown and a crown made of lighted candles. She goes from room to room, waking her siblings and parents while serving coffee and breakfast buns. Since mid-December is often marked by the longest nights of the year, the light of St. Lucia's candles are meant to bring light to the darkness.

Today, some Swedish Americans continue to celebrate Saint Lucia's Day both in church and in their homes. The beauty of the custom has been adopted by some other cultures, too.

Chapter FOUR

The Swedish-American Culture

SOMETIMES IT IS HARD TO IMAGINE WHAT THE United States would be like without the influence of Swedish Americans. These imaginative people showed perseverance and initiative, making them leaders in American society.

Pultizer Prize–winning author Carl Sandburg

The Swedes who settled in America during the 19th and early 20th centuries went on to have families. These new generations of Swedish Americans have given much to the United States.

One of the most famous second-generation Swedish Americans is Carl Sandburg, a writer

who grew up in Illinois. He was known for his poetry as well as for his books about Abraham Lincoln, *The Prairie Years* (two volumes published in 1926) and *The War Years* (four volumes published in 1939), for which he won a **Pulitzer Prize** in 1940. His *Complete Poems* won a Pulitzer in 1951.

Edgar Bergen and his puppet, Charlie McCarthy

Entertainer Edgar Bergen was best known as a ventriloquist and charmed many audiences with his puppet, Charlie McCarthy. Bergen was born in Chicago in 1903 to Swedish parents. He and his wife, Nellie, later had a daughter, Candace Bergen, who became a popular star in films and on television.

Charles Lindbergh, the first pilot to fly solo across the Atlantic Ocean

Pilot Charles Lindbergh, the son of a Swede, worked on the family farm in Minnesota. In 1927, he made history by becoming the first person to fly solo across the Atlantic Ocean.

Swedish Americans are responsible for founding many churches throughout the United States. Many of these are

Swedish Americans follow the faith of the Lutheran Church as well as other denominations.

Lutheran, but they also include Methodist, Episcopalian, Congregationalist, Baptist, and other **denominations**. These citizens celebrated the religious freedom in their new home and were eager to provide places of worship for their communities. Many of these churches still exist today, and some even conduct services in Swedish.

In the kitchen, Sweden contributed the tradition of the *smorgasbord,* which is a selection

The smorgasbord, a buffet with a wide array of foods, originated in Sweden.

of cold and hot foods usually served as a buffet. Smorgasbords are often featured on holidays, in restaurants, and on board cruise ships.

When Swedes first arrived in the United States, many worked on farms and on railroads. They helped to settle the American West and played a vital role in the growth of the young nation. Today, some Swedish Americans are still farmers, but there are also Swedish-American lawyers and politicians, doctors and scientists. They have inherited the deter-mination of their **ancestors** and they work hard. Though they were born in America, many of them still embrace the traditions

Some Swedish Americans are still farmers, but others have pursued a variety of professions.

Interesting Fact

▸ Mans Olsson Lindbergh, the grandfather of pilot Charles Lindbergh, was a Swedish immigrant who served in the Union army during the Civil War (1861–1865).

27

of their grandparents and great-grandparents. For example, they may still worship at the Lutheran Church and enjoy smorgasbords on special occasions. For them, being Swedish-American is just that, a wonderful blending of two special cultures.

A young Swedish American in traditional clothing of Sweden

6000 B.C. The first settlers come to Sweden.

829 Christianity is introduced to Sweden.

c. 1540 Lutheranism becomes Sweden's official religion.

1638 Swedes first come to the American colonies and establish New Sweden.

1655 New Sweden is lost to the Dutch.

1809 Sweden loses land from Finland and its own country to Russia; King Gustav IV is forced from power.

1814 Sweden gains the land of Norway from Denmark.

1839 John Ericsson moves to America.

1840s Swedish immigrants begin coming to America in large numbers.

1841 Gustav Unonius moves to America and writes letters to Swedish friends about the country's beauty and promise.

1862 The Homestead Act gives 160 acres (65 hectares) to people willing to settle in certain western states.

1867–1886 Harsh economic conditions in Sweden cause more its people to emigrate to the United States.

1892 Ellis Island opens.

1905 Norway and Sweden dissolve their union.

1927 Pilot Charles Lindbergh becomes the first person to fly solo across the Atlantic Ocean.

1929 The Great Depression begins and the wave of Swedish immigration nearly stops.

1940 Carl Sandburg wins a Pulitzer Prize for Abraham Lincoln: The War Years.

1951 Carl Sandburg wins a Pulitzer Prize for his Complete Poems.

2000 Sweden separates church and state, so Lutheranism is no longer the official religion.

Glossary Terms

alliance (uh-LYE-uhnss)
An alliance is a bond between countries to protect their common interests. Sweden formed an alliance with Russia and Great Britain during the Napoleonic Wars.

ancestors (AN-sess-turs)
Ancestors are relatives who lived before the present generation, such as grandparents. Today's Swedish Americans have inherited the determination of their ancestors.

democratic (dem-uh-KRAT-ik)
A democratic government is controlled by its citizens and promotes equality for all people. Swedes found the democratic government of the United States to be appealing.

denominations (di-nom-uh-NAY-shuhns)
Denominations are various religious communities. Swedish Americans now belong to a number of denominations.

descendants (di-SEND-uhnts)
Descendants are grandchildren and other relatives of previous generations. Descendants of New Sweden settlers fought in the Revolutionary War.

droughts (DROWTS)
Droughts are long spells of very dry weather. Droughts ruined many harvests in Sweden, leading some farmers to try their luck in America.

Great Depression (GRAYT di-PRESH-uhn)
The Great Depression is an era in U.S. history (1929–1942) marked by poverty and unemployment. The wave of European immigration slowed when the Great Depression began.

immigrants (IM-uh-gruhnts)
Immigrants are people who settle in a new country. Swedish immigrants traveled to America on huge cargo ships.

memoirs (MEM-whars)
Memoirs are writings about one's life. Gustav Unonius published his memoirs when he returned to Sweden.

meteorologist (mee-tee-ur-OL-oh-jist))
A meteorologist is a person who specializes in meteorology, the study of earth's climate and weather. Carl-Gustaf Rossby was a meteorologist who studied jet streams.

Napoleonic Wars (na-pole-ee-ON-ik wors)
The Napoleonic Wars were battles fought by Napoléon Bonaparte and his army to gain more land for France. Life in Sweden changed dramatically after the Napoleonic Wars.

Pulitzer Prize (puh-LIT-sur PRIZE)
Pulitzer Prizes are given each year to award excellence in writing. Carl Sandburg won Pulitzers in 1940 and 1951.

union activist (YOON-yuhn AK-ti-vist)
A union activist is someone who tries to get better working conditions for union members. Joe Hill was a well-known union activist.

For Further INFORMATION

Web Sites

Visit our homepage for lots of links about Swedish Americans:
http://www.childsworld.com/links.html

Note to Parents, Teachers, and Librarians:
We routinely verify our Web links to make sure they're safe,
active sites—so encourage your readers to check them out!

Books

McGill, Allyson. *The Swedish Americans.* New York: Chelsea House, 1997.

Meltzer, Milton. *Carl Sandburg: A Biography.* New York: Twenty-First Century Books, 1999.

Shaw, Janet Beeler. *Meet Kirsten: An American Girl.* New York: Pleasant Company Publications, 1986.

Winter, Jeanette. *Klara's New World.* New York: Alfred A. Knopf, 1992.

Places to Visit or Contact

American Swedish Historical Museum
1900 Pattison Avenue
South Philadelphia, PA 19145
215-389-1776

The American Swedish Institute
2600 Park Avenue
Minneapolis, MN 55407
612-871-4907

Swedish American Museum Center
5211 North Clark
Chicago, IL 60640
773-728-8111

Index

Ann-Margret, 21
art, 17

Bergen, Candace, 25
Bergen, Edgar, 25
Bergman, Ingrid, 21
Bishop Hill community, 10
Bonaparte, Napoléon, 8

Castle Garden, 13
Chicago, Illinois, 14, 19
Civil War, 12, 20, 27
Complete Poems (Carl Sandburg), 25

Duluth, Minnesota, 14

Ellis Island, 13
employment, 14, 16, 18, 27
entertainment, 21
Ericsson, John, 20

farming, 8, 10, 14–15, 18, 19, 27
foods, 10, 26–27, 28
Fountain of Faith (Carl Milles), 17
Fountain of the Muses (Carl Milles), 17
Franklin, Benjamin, 7

Garbo, Greta, 21
Great Depression, 16
Gustav III, king of Sweden, 7
Gustav IV, king of Sweden, 8

Hemlandet (newspaper), 7, 19
Hill, Joe, 21
Homestead Act, 14
Hoving, Walter, 21

immigration examinations, 13

Jansson, Eric, 10
jet streams, 16

Lindbergh, Charles, 25, 27
Lindbergh, Mans Olsson, 27
literature, 24–25
Lutheran Church, 9, 26

Meeting of the Waters fountain (Carl Milles), 17
Merrimac (warship), 20
Milles, Carl, 17
Millesgärden, 17
Milwaukee, Wisconsin, 14, 19
Minnesota, 14, 19
Monitor (warship), 20

names, 15
Napoleonic Wars, 7–8
New Sweden, 6
New Uppsala, 11
New York, 12, 13–14, 15
newspapers, 7, 19–20

Pietists, 9
population, 8, 14, 19
Präireblomman (journal), 20
The Prairie Years (Carl Sandburg), 25
Princeton (warship), 20
publishing, 7, 19–20

railroads, 27
religion, 9–10, 25–26, 28
Revolutionary War, 6
Rossby, Carl-Gustaf, 16

Saint Lucia's Day, 22
Sandburg, Carl, 24–25
smorgasbords, 26-27, 28
Svenska Amerikanare (newspaper), 19–20
Swanson, Carl, 21
Swede Town, 19
Sweden, 7–10, 15

Unonius, Charlotte, 11
Unonius, Gustav, 11

Valkyrian (journal), 20
voyage, 12, 14

The War Years (Carl Sandburg), 25
Warren, Earl, 28
World War I, 15